LVT(4) Amtrac

Written by David Doyle

In Action

Cover Art by Don Greer

Line Illustrations by Todd Sturgell

(Front Cover) Originally conceived as a hurricane rescue vehicle, the Landing Vehicle, Tank (LVT) rose to fame during the campaigns in the Pacific. In addition to the Marines in the Pacific, the U.S. Army used the vehicle as well, both in the Pacific and in Europe, and Commonwealth nations used the vehicles in multiple theaters.

(Back Cover) With its rear loading ramp, the LVT(4) was among the most versatile and numerous of the amphibious tractors (amtracs). This version was produced by Food Machinery Corporation (FMC), Graham-Paige, and St. Louis Car Company.

About the In Action® Series

In Action books, despite the title of the genre, are books that trace the development of a single type of aircraft, armored vehicle, or ship from prototype to the final production variant. Experimental or "one-off" variants can also be included. Our first *In Action* book was printed in 1971.

Hardcover ISBN 978-0-89747-754-3
Softcover ISBN 978-0-89747-755-0

Proudly printed in the U.S.A.
Copyright 2014 Squadron/Signal Publications
1115 Crowley Drive, Carrollton, TX 75006-1312 U.S.A.

Military/Combat Photographs and Snapshots

If you have any photos of aircraft, armor, soldiers, or ships of any nation, particularly wartime snapshots, why not share them with us and help make Squadron/Signal's books all the more interesting and complete in the future? Any photograph sent to us will be copied and returned. Electronic images are preferred. The donor will be fully credited for any photos used. Please send them to:

Squadron/Signal Publications
1115 Crowley Drive
Carrollton, TX 75006-1312 U.S.A.
www.SquadronSignalPublications.com

(Title Page) Gunners at the ready on the side-mounted .50-caliber machine guns, an early LVT(4) comes ashore near the FMC plant located in the area of Riverside, California. (Patton Museum)

Acknowledgments

David Harper had an insatiable thirst for information relating to the LVT. Not only did he frequently delve into archives seeking materials, also asked his friends to do the same for him. Through the years, whenever I came across LVT materials, I would gladly forward them to Dave. In time he began working on this, his dream book. His untimely death prevented him from completing this volume, and it has been my privilege to carry this forward. Joining me in this task were many friends and associates, to whom I am indebted, including Tom Kailbourn, Scott Taylor, Steve Zaloga, the staffs of the many institutions recognized in the photo credits, the editorial team of Squadron, and most of all my lovely wife Denise.

Introduction

Andrew Jackson Higgins brought the troops to Europe in his LCVP, but it was Donald Roebling who took them to the Pacific islands.

In fact, General Holland M. ("Howling Mad") Smith, USMC, said: "The development of the amphibian tractor, or LVT, which began in the middle 1930s, provided the solution and was one of the most important modern technical contributions to ship-to-shore operations. Without these landing vehicles our amphibious offensive in the Pacific would have been impossible."

Roebling, whose great-grandfather, John Augustus Roebling, designed the Brooklyn Bridge, and whose grandfather, Washington Roebling, built the famed structure, designed what would become the LVT as a swamp rescue vehicle in the aftermath of a 1928 Florida hurricane.

Donald's father, John A. Roebling II, was Washington Roebling's trusted assistant, and as the 20th Century began he was managing the Roebling family wire rope business. After guiding the firm through World War I, John's interests turned to finance and banking. By the 1920s he had achieved fame as a financier and philanthropist, and had built a winter home in Lake Placid, Florida. This location would be key to his son's creation of the amphibious tractor, dubbed "the Alligator" by his son's workers.

John's employees related how many of the area residents survived the initial hurricane only to succumb to snakes, alligators, and drowning when rescue workers were unable to reach them in a timely manner. Moved by this misfortune, John hired his mechanically talented but languid son – who lived in Florida and occupied himself with a construction company building mansions – to devise a vehicle capable of traversing swampy terrain.

Donald and his team began working on the project in 1932, hoping to have an operational vehicle in 1933. Despite their enthusiastic efforts, it was 1935 before a running prototype was completed, and that vehicle was plagued by slow speed and oft-breaking tracks – as were subsequent improved prototypes. It would be 1937, and Roebling's fourth prototype, before a vehicle that met Donald and John Roeblings' expectations of speed and reliability was completed.

The odd vehicle attracted the interest of *Life* magazine, which ran an article and photos of the vehicle in its 4 October 1937 issue. Through good fortune, this article was noticed by Rear Admiral Edward C. Kalbfus, who at a party showed the feature to Major General Louis McCarty Little, USMC, who was extremely interested in the machine.

Despite opposition from many inside the Corps, as well as in the Navy, a test vehicle was finally purchased from Roebling in November 1940. On trial, the vehicle proved its worth, and fulfilled the Corps requirements. Various engines were tried in the Alligators, including an 85-horsepower Ford V-8 and a 95-horsepower Mercury V-8. The vehicles pioneered methods of manufacturing lightweight, buoyant vehicles, being largely constructed of aluminum.

A contract for 200 vehicles was awarded to Roebling in February 1940. However, the trial vehicles had been assembled in Roebling's home garage – ill suited to filling such a contract. Roebling turned to the nearby Dunedin, Florida, Food Machinery Corporation (FMC) plant, which had fabricated some of the parts for his prototypes, to produce the vehicles, by then known as the LVT(1).

Alligator orders exceeded even FMC's production capacity, and a new plant was built in Lakeland – fittingly by Donald Roebling's construction company. The earnings from this construction project were the only profit the Roebling family made from the LVT venture – the track design patent being transferred to the government as an act of patriotism. The family, whose New Jersey wire rope plants had burned during World War I – in what was believed to be the act of saboteurs – felt that it was their patriotic duty to provide U.S. troops with the best and safest means of amphibious operations possible.

Improvements to the original FMC-built vehicle known as the LVT(2) resulted in the LVT(4). This series of amphibious tracked vehicles (amtracs) were developed from the original tracked amphibious vehicles built by Donald Roebling, known as the LVT(1) or Alligator.

One of the first major enhancements to the new amtrac series was the fact that FMC chose to utilize existing components of proven designs that were already in the military supply system. These included the Continental nine-cylinder radial gasoline W670-9A engine and transmission used in the M3 Stuart light tank series, along with other

In the 1930s, Donald Roebling, great-grandson of John A. Roebling, who designed the Brooklyn Bridge, developed a series of experimental amphibious vehicles specifically designed to perform rescue operations in swampy areas. These vehicles, dubbed the Alligator, were propelled on land and in water by continuous tracks fitted with large, angled cleats. Eventually, the Alligators attained speeds of 8.6 miles per hour on water and 25 miles per hour on land. Shown here is one of Roebling's Alligators. (USMC)

components like the crew seats, driver's controls, intercom, radios, optics and electrical systems. Despite these efforts, there was considerable new engineering and design work in the vehicles. Since the original vehicle requirements called for a machine that could move troops and supplies from ship to shore, it was never really intended to operate in an assault or combat role. The early designs were built of mild steel and included no armor plating or defensive weapons of any type. The Amphibious Assault Doctrine used so successfully by the Allies in the Pacific Theatre during WWII was still being developed early in the war and into 1943.

After the campaigns fought in 1942 in the Solomon Islands at places like Guadalcanal and up through the New Guinea Islands chain, where amtracs played many diverse and important roles, the LVT was seen as a very capable addition to the Allied arsenal. In order to employ the amtracs in the amphibious assault role, it was necessary to add externally mounted plates of armor to protect the front cab and the rear-mounted engine compartment and fuel tanks.

Defensive armament was added in the form of several Browning .30- and .50-caliber machine guns. The guns were mounted on a common skate rail system used on other American vehicles like the M2-M3 Half-Track series and White Scout Cars. All of the FMC LVTs before the LVT(4) were rear-engine designs, a feature that made the cargo compartment smaller and harder to load and unload since access to the cargo compartment had to be made from either side of the vehicle, climbing or loading everything over the six-foot high side pontoons.

Engineers at FMC decided to relocate the rear-mounted engine forward in the vehicle, just behind the driver's compartment. This arrangement allowed for a larger cargo compartment, and a ramp installed in the rear of the vehicle made access to the cargo compartment much easier and allowed for pre-loaded pallets to be quickly loaded and unloaded. Several documents from the earliest days of the LVT(4) project referred to the vehicle as a "Modified LVT(2) with Stern Ramp," before the official designation of Landing Vehicle Tracked Model 4 was assigned.

As with any bureaucracy, changes or modifications took longer than they should have to show up on the production line. The first production run of the LVT(4) was a completely unarmored version again made of mild steel. As with the earlier LVT models, kits of armor plates were quickly designed and manufactured to be added to these early production LVT(4)s. A completely armored cab piece was developed to replace the vehicle's original unarmored cab. The first armored cab did away with the front windows and instead had a small hinged flap located in front of the driver. A later WWII armored cab was designed that eliminated the driver's side hinged flap and instead had four armored glass view ports located around the front surfaces for the driver and assistant driver. The assistant driver's position was also provided with a Browning .30-caliber machine gun in a ball socket mount for vehicle defense.

Ultimately, thousands of these Roebling-designed Alligators would be produced in a variety of styles by companies such as FMC, Borg-Warner, Graham-Paige, and St. Louis Car Company. Descendants of these vehicles continue to see service today around the world.

An article on the Alligator in the 4 October 1937 issue of *Life* magazine intrigued a U.S. Navy admiral, who made inquiries into the possible military use of the vehicle. In early 1940 the Marine Corps contracted with Roebling for an Alligator, receiving one example, the fifth one constructed, later that year. This Alligator is seen coming ashore at Culebra, Puerto Rico, in November 1940 during Fleet Exercise Seven. The enclosed cab was well forward on the vehicle and had three glass windshields. (USMC)

An Alligator comes ashore in a swamp. The cleats on the tracks that helped propel the vehicle through water would also provide extra traction on land in scenarios such as this one. Along the port side of the hull is a fender, supported by numerous triangular brackets. In the bulkhead at the rear of the cab is a single large entry door, shown open. At the rear of the open cargo compartment of the vehicle is the engine compartment, with what appears to be an engine exhaust and muffler on top. (USMC)

An LVT (1) undergoes lifting tests. Like any other tracked military vehicle, the LVT(1) was fitted with lifting eyes. Often, the vehicle would be lifted to load it onto transport vehicles, and in some cases it would be lifted over the side of a transport vessel during a seaborne operation. The curved shapes of the cleats on the tracks are particularly visible in this view. Painted in white on the vehicle are an identification star and the number 2H 4. Mooring posts, headlights with guards, and a towing clevis are apparent on the front of the vehicle. (National Archives)

Bearing a sinuous camouflage pattern, an LVT(1) conducts exercises on a beach, water dripping from the track cleats. Unlike the aluminum-construction Alligator, the LVT(1) was constructed of steel. On the sides of the hull were watertight pontoons, to enhance flotation. This example had six steps arranged in two rows indented into the sponsons; some LVT(1)s had four steps per side. There was a square window was on each side of the cab: the port window appears as a black square in this photo. (National Archives)

As United States involvement in World War II became inevitable, the Food Machinery Corporation (FMC) received a contract to study optimal propulsion designs for amphibian vehicles. Shortly after the United States entered the conflict, FMC won a U.S. Navy contract to build 200 amphibious tractors similar in design to the Alligator. Designated "Landing Vehicle, Tracked Mk. I," also known as the LVT(1), a number of these vehicles are shown on FMC's Dunedin, Florida, assembly line. (National Archives)

An improvement over the LVT(1), the LVT(2) featured a lengthened hull with extended bow and stern, a lower cab, and pontoons that did not cover the suspension and track-support rollers. Whereas the drive sprockets of the LVT(1) were at the rear, those of the LVT(2) were at the front. There were other, more subtle, changes in the LVT(2), including a redesigned torsion-spring suspension, replacing the LVT(1)'s rigid suspension, and new tracks with hermetically sealed bearings. (Patton Museum)

From 1943 to 1944, FMC produced 450 examples of the LVT(A)2, similar to the LVT(2) but with ½-inch armor on the cab front and ¼-inch armor on the front, sides, and rear of the hull and the sides of the cab. Like the LVT(2), the LVT(A)2 was powered by the Continental W-670-9A air-cooled, seven-cylinder radial engine: a reliable engine used on the late M3 light tank and M3A1 light tank. A single window cover was provided on the front of the cab for the driver. (Patton Museum)

Development

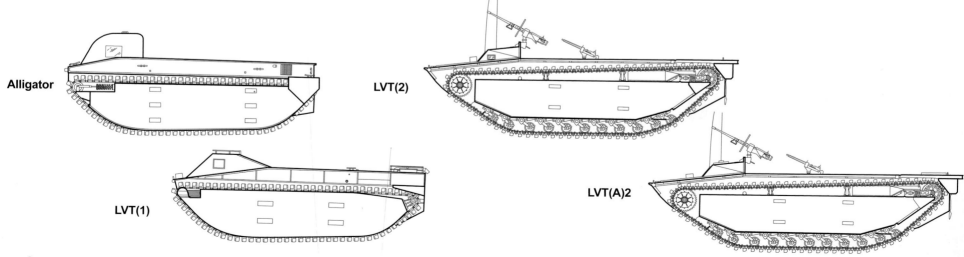

Alligator

LVT(2)

LVT(1)

LVT(A)2

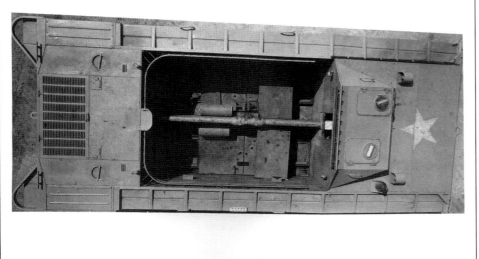

The forerunner of the LVT(4) was the LVT(2), and the armored derivative, the LVT(A)2. On these, the engine was located in a compartment at the rear of the vehicle, just aft of the cargo compartment. Troops and cargo were loaded and unloaded from the sides of this version of the amtrac. Running down the full length of the center line of the cargo compartment was the drive train connecting to the transmission located in the front cab between the driver's and assistant driver's seats. (Patton Museum)

The LVT(4) was basically a heavily modified LVT(2), with the engine relocated to the front of the cargo compartment, directly behind the front cab. This allowed for a much larger cargo compartment. A rear ramp was added to make it easier to load and unload cargo and provide a better egress option for the infantrymen who could also be carried in the vehicle. (Patton Museum)

Although LVTs had been employed in several operations as cargo and troop transports before the fall of 1943, the Tarawa invasion in November 1943 was the first major combat test of these vehicles. As seen on this LVT(2) photographed from a ship during the invasion of Tarawa, ¼-inch-thick armor plates had been installed on the fronts and sides of the cabs prior to the invasion in New Zealand. A clear view is provided of the interior of the cargo compartment, including the drive shaft. (USMC)

GIs file onto an LVT(4) on a beach. Whereas previous versions of the LVT with rear-mounted engines required personnel to climb up the sides of the vehicles to enter the cargo compartment, the rear ramp of the LVT(4) made it much easier to enter or exit the vehicle. This example is a nonstandard LVT(4), possibly a prototype, with a "dip" in the gunwale, or sponson. (National Archives)

The early unarmored versions of the LVT(4) were made of mild steel. The need for additional armor was quickly discovered and several add-on armor plate kits were designed and added to all of the early vehicles. Above each front window, in the cab roof, was a solid-metal hinged escape hatch, one each for the driver and assistant driver. (USMC)

Also featuring on early unarmored versions of the LVT(4) were the two front cab hinged escape hatches. With their standard glass windows, these were quickly found to be a major weak point in combat. Two solid metal hinged escape hatches, one each for the driver and the assistant driver, were located in the cab roof above the front windows. (USMC)

LVT(4) Armored Cab Development

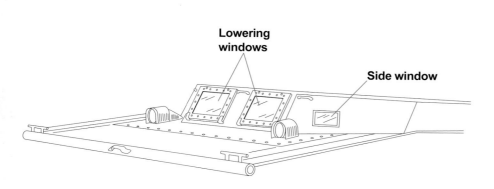

Lowering windows

Side window

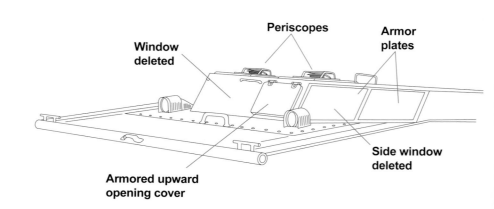

Periscopes

Armor plates

Window deleted

Armored upward opening cover

Side window deleted

The LVT(4) was a slightly taller and longer vehicle than the earlier variants. Its new larger cargo compartment enabled it to carry more troops and supplies, and the rear ramp made access much easier. (USMC)

A rear ramp was added to make it easier to load and unload cargo and provide a better egress option for the infantrymen who could also be carried in the vehicle. This particular variant of the LVT(4) is the first model produced with the early unarmored cab and no add-on armor plating. (USMC)

The tracks of the LVT(4) featured W-shaped cleats. It was determined that these cleats provided better directional stability than the curved cleats of former models of the LVT. The ramp did not constitute a single plate, but rather was a watertight structure designed to assist with the vehicle's flotation. (USMC)

The LVT(2) series had the engine located in the rear of the vehicle. Moving the engine forward and adding a rear ramp to the LVT(4) was a significant improvement in terms of accessibility and efficient use of the cargo compartment. (USMC)

An early LVT(4) is viewed from the front. The "pipe" running horizontally across the front of the hull with a tow eye at the center was not a bumper, but bilge-pump outlets. Two headlights were mounted on the front deck, protected by C-shaped guards. The light-colored cleats on the tracks were instrumental in propelling the vehicle through water and for providing traction on sand and muddy terrain. (USMC)

A direct view of the left side of an early production LVT(4), showing its rather sleek lines and complete chain-type track drive system. All versions of the LVT(4) were produced with the spoked idler seen here. Only one step pocket was incorporated into the pontoon face and the drive sprocket was the same drive sprocket that was used on all FMC-designed LVTs. (USMC)

A view of an early LVT(4) produced by the St. Louis Car Company illustrates the layout of the vehicle as viewed from above. Visible toward the bottom of the rear half of the inner side panel of the left pontoon is a large, removable panel covering the left fuel tank, to the front of which are manholes providing access to the two batteries. The layout of the inner panel of the right pontoon of the LVT(4) had an access panel for the right fuel tank, but there were no manholes or covers for batteries on that side. (USMC)

The ramp is open and the engine access panels have been removed from the forward cargo compartment wall, showing the radial engine. The rectangular openings on either side of the engine compartment are passageways leading from the cargo compartment to the front cab interior. Usually only the left one was kept open, as in this photo. Visible on the side walls of the cargo compartment are the add-on armor plates protecting the fuel cells and cargo interior at the vehicle's waterline. (Washington University)

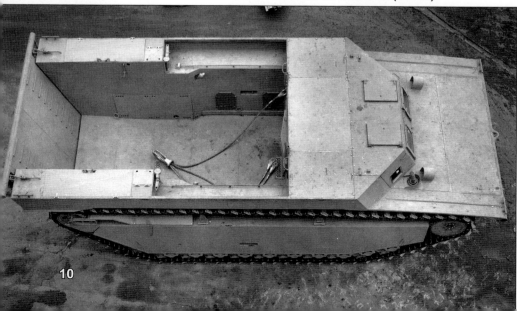

The first production run of the new LVT(4) began in late1942. These vehicles were made entirely of mild steel and featured many improvements over earlier LVT models. The early mooring posts and pulling staple are holdovers from the former types that were soon changed on mid and late production versions. (USMC)

The Continental W670-9A radial gasoline engine was the engine chosen for all of the FMC-designed LVTs. The same engine was also used in the M3 Stuart light tank series, a fact that facilitated engine maintenance and changes and made it easier to keep spare parts moving smoothly through the supply chain. (Washington University)

The engine compartment of an LVT(4) is viewed from aft, providing a glimpse of the Continental W-670-9A air-cooled, seven-cylinder radial engine and its mount. This engine had a displacement of 668 cubic inches and produced a maximum of 250 horsepower at 2,400 r.p.m. (Washington University)

Suspended from an engine sling, a Continental W-670-9A engine displays its maze of hoses, pulleys, belts, and accessories. The belt is connected to the generator toward the bottom left of the engine. Mounted on the engine support beam, the engine could be fairly rapidly installed or removed from the vehicle. (Washington University)

A Continental W-670-9A radial engine from an LVT(4) is viewed from above, displaying several of the cylinders and the exhaust manifold. The mufflers were contained in the engine compartment, as was the transmission oil cooler. The engine was coupled to a five-speed Synchromesh transmission. (Washington University)

Very soon after the introduction of the LVT(4) came the realization that the lack of any type of armor protection was resulting in a great number of human combat casualties and catastrophic losses of the vehicles themselves. The engineers at FMC came up with series of add-on armor plates that could be added to all of the vehicles currently in production as well as the vehicles already issued in the field. (Naval History and Heritage Command)

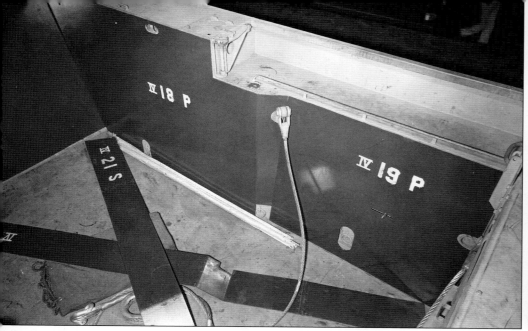

A complete armor kit was designed that covered all of the walls of the cargo compartment, including the ramp, with ½-inch armor plate. The kit proved to be too heavy, though, adversely affecting capability and performance. (Naval History and Heritage Command)

The kit armor applied to the LTV(4)'s ramp is shown in this photo from Mare Island Navy Yard dated 22 February 1944. Lateral cleats were welded to the armor to provide a nonslip tread. (Naval History and Heritage Command)

The only armor plates added to the cargo compartment interior on the LVT(4) modified at Mare Island in February 1944 were these strips fitted along the water level. Plates and brackets were sprayed with dark-colored paint. (Naval History and Heritage Command)

The kit armor on the starboard longitudinal bulkhead of an LTV(4)'s cargo compartment is displayed. Toward the bottom of the bulkhead are two tie-down rings. The lowered ramp is to the bottom right. (Naval History and Heritage Command)

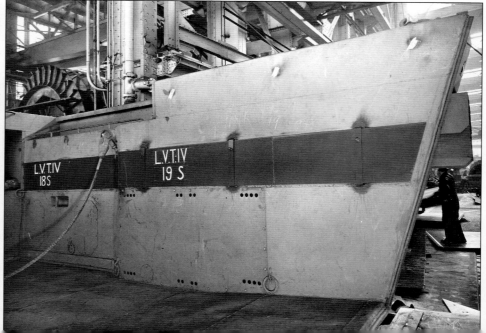

The driver's station on the port side of the cab includes a padded seat, steering levers, gearshift lever with lock button on the grip, a small instrument panel, and a compass (right). To the lower right is the transmission, and to the front is the final-drive tunnel. (Naval History and Heritage Command)

The starboard side of the interior of the cab of an early LVT(4) is viewed from the driver's perspective. The assistant driver's window has a dark-colored frame and is flanked by grab handles. A smaller window is on the side of the cab. (Naval History and Heritage Command)

This early-production LVT(4) is going through its sea trials. The white markings on the side of the pontoon indicate the vehicle's displacement at different speeds with different weight loads being carried. The hollow pipe on the front edge of the bow is the bilge-pump discharge outlet. This vehicle also carries the very early (pre-production) "pointed" suspension brackets. (Patton Museum)

Carrying a complete artillery piece and its crew was possible with the improved design of the LVT(4). Additional vehicles would carry the ammunition for the guns; often the ammo was carried in DUKWs for delivery to the gun crews in the field. (National Archives)

Because of the larger cargo compartment and better access to it, for the first time an LVT could carry small vehicles and palletized cargo loads. Here an LVT(4) is undergoing tests to assess its ability to bring a jeep ashore. To the right, a film cameraman is documenting the exercise. (Washington University)

It was a tight squeeze, and the barrel had to be set at full elevation for the piece to fit, but this 105mm howitzer was ready for delivery to a beachhead. With a cargo compartment capacity of 541 cubic feet, the LVT(4) had a decided advantage over the LVT(2)'s 364 cubic feet. (Patton Museum)

The LVT(4) was also tested as a candidate for a rocket-equipped vehicle. These small anti-beach defense systems were eventually mounted on an assortment of different vehicles, including LCMs, LCVPs, DUKWs, LCIs, LCTs, PT-Boats, and trucks, as well as LVTs. (USMC)

The first major upgrade to the LVT(4) series was the addition of an all-armored cab for the driver's and assistant driver's positions. Included in this upgrade was a series of add-on armor panels to be installed on the sides of the front cab and the bow of the vehicle. The bow armor is visible in this photo; the top of this armor extended above the bilge-pump outlet, with gaps in the armor for the tow eye and mooring bits. The inside faces of the crew hatches are painted interior gloss white and not the vehicle's exterior color, as was common with tanks. (USMC)

Viewed from overhead, this LVT(4) features an early armored cab with one front viewing port. Rotating periscopes are visible through the two open escape doors on the cab roof. On the cab's starboard side is an antenna mount surrounded by a splash guard. Two Browning M2 .50-caliber machine guns and two Browning M1919 .30-caliber machine guns are present. (TACOM LCMC History Office)

Seen inside the cargo compartment of an LVT(4) are two .30-caliber machine gun mounts on the sides and the two .50-caliber mounts at the front of the compartment. On the port longitudinal bulkhead, to the left, is a hand crank for manually operating the ramp. An M1 carbine is stowed on the forward bulkhead. (Patton Museum)

The port side of an LVT(4) is seen at Aberdeen Proving Ground on 6 October 1944. This vehicle has been modified with rectangular appliqué armor plates fastened to the pontoon adjacent to the driver's compartment and at the lower aft corner of the pontoon. The sprocket, idler, and 11 bogie wheels are also visible. (USMC)

At the forward starboard corner of the cargo compartment is a collapsible rack for storing ammunition boxes, shown folded down in this February 1945 photograph. To the extreme left is the forward lifting eye on the starboard side of the vehicle. Also present are five-gallon liquid containers, a sledgehammer, a tow rope, and ammunition boxes strapped to a rail. (Patton Museum)

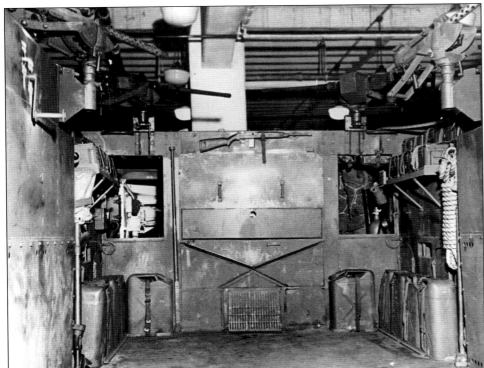

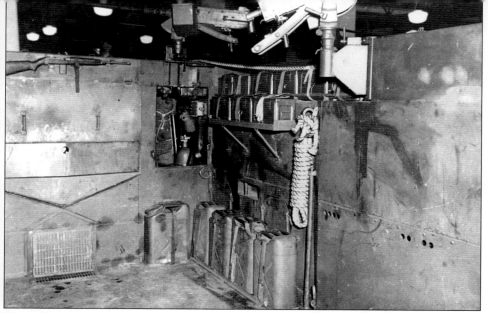

The port longitudinal bulkhead of an LVT(4) appears to the left, while to the right is the forward bulkhead of the cargo compartment, which also served as the rear bulkhead of the engine compartment. The removable hand crank to the left is mounted on the "lower ramp" fitting, aft of and slightly above which is the "raise ramp" fitting. (Patton Museum)

The port side of the cargo compartment of an LVT(4) is viewed from atop the engine compartment. Stored vertically at the center is a machine gun tripod, above and aft of which is a .30-caliber machine gun mount. A .50-caliber machine gun is at the top of the sponson, above the ammunition boxes. (Patton Museum)

The forward starboard corner of an LVT(4) cargo compartment is depicted. To the left is the access panel for the engine. To the right of that panel on the engine compartment bulkhead is a small compartment for stowing equipment; among other things, a canteen and what appears to be a fire extinguisher are visible inside it. (Patton Museum)

The starboard side of the cargo compartment is observed from the top of the engine compartment, showing the collapsible ammunition rack in use. This LVT(4) was built by Graham-Paige, a car builder that produced vehicles for the military during the war. In addition to that firm and FMC, the St. Louis Car Company also produced LVT(4)s. (Patton Museum)

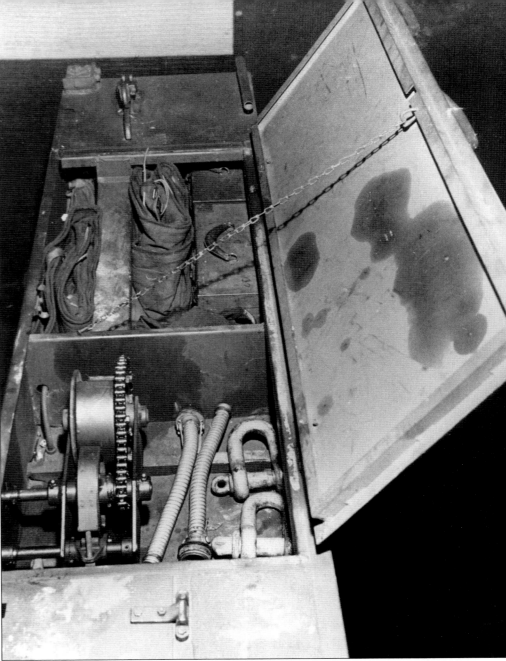

Built into the sponsons of the LVT(4) were stowage compartments with doors on top, hinged on the outboard side of the vehicle. Several sheet-metal dividers were placed laterally in the compartments. Among the items visible in this starboard compartment are a flashlight and canned goods. (Patton Museum)

The sponson stowage compartment on the port side of an LVT(4) cargo compartment is viewed with its grease-stained door open. In the closest bay of the compartment is the hand-operated mechanism for operating the ramp. Also present in that bay are two towing clevises and a couple of flexible fuel filler hoses. (Patton Museum)

The port way, or the small, doorless compartment to the left of the engine compartment, is viewed from the cargo compartment. Two storage boxes are mounted to the left; to the right of the lower box, just inside the way, is a vehicular lifting eye. Within the way is an electrical box and a binoculars case. (Patton Museum)

The starboard way of an LVT(4) is viewed from the forward starboard corner of the cargo compartment. Among the pieces of equipment stowed inside the way are a fire extinguisher (lower right) and a lubrication and maintenance chart (lower left). The forward starboard lifting eye is at the lower right of the way. (Patton Museum)

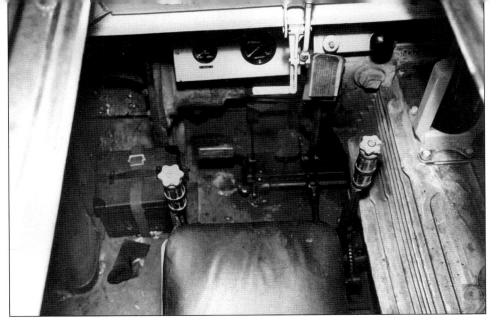

The driver's compartment of a Graham-Paige-built LVT(4) is viewed through the escape hatch atop the cab, showing the upholstered seat and steering levers. At the top is the instrument panel, and the transmission is to the right. To the left, a small box with a handle is secured to the floor with a webbing strap. (Patton Museum)

The assistant driver's compartment is viewed from the driver's compartment, with an M1 carbine stowed in holders. On the aft bulkhead (right) are a periscope and fire extinguisher. The assistant driver also served as the vehicle's radioman, operating a radio set in watertight containers in his compartment. (Patton Museum)

The port side of the driver's compartment of a Graham-Paige LVT(4) is shown. Above the vertically stored M3 .45-caliber submachine gun is the driver's radio control box. To the right is part of the electrical panel, which included switches for the starter, generator, lights, and other electrical systems. (Patton Museum)

A February 1945 view through the assistant driver's hatch of a Graham-Paige LVT(4) shows the right side of the transmission (left) and the watertight lockers holding radio equipment (right). The locking handles for the radio locker doors are visible. To the front of the compartment is the final-drive tunnel's right side. (Patton Museum)

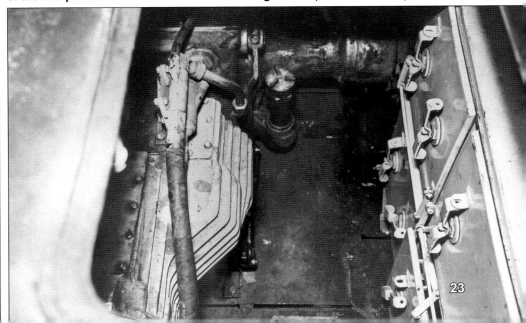

Late Production Vehicles

The final production versions of the LVT(4) incorporated all of the prior modifications introduced in the series as well as a few new ones. A redesigned armored cab featured four armored glass view ports lining the front and side cab surfaces. A Browning M1919 .30-caliber machine gun was mounted in a ball socket in the front cab in the assistant driver's position and two overhead escape hatches were modified for the driver and assistant driver.

The periscope was deleted from the driver's escape hatch, due to the addition of the new view ports surrounding his position. The assistant driver's overhead escape hatch retained a periscope for use in operating the machine gun that had been added to this position. A new-style mooring post was added, along with an improved pulling staple, armor package, redesigned ramp, water boxes, and in a few cases, new return roller mounts, plus an improved tow-cable storage arrangement and a new towing hook design.

Late in WWII several nations showed interest in purchasing the LVT(4). The French requested that a new escape hatch be added in the left side pontoon face. This addition necessitated that a small round glass view port be incorporated into the hatch, so that the crew could see the level of water that the vehicle was sitting in before attempting to open that hatch. This modification was introduced into the production line in early 1945 and some of these modified LVT(4)s were issued to American troops before the war ended.

This LVT(4) produced by the St. Louis Car Company exhibits late-model features, including a late-type armored cab enclosure with openings for vision blocks, a ball mount for a .30-caliber machine gun, and a mooring post mounted at the center of the forward deck. A Plexiglas dome is visible over one of the periscopes. (Washington University)

A frontal view of a late-model LVT(4) made by the St. Louis Car Company shows the armor on the lower front of the hull, with the top of the armor wrapping around the bilge discharge pipe running across the front edge of the hull. The vision blocks are fitted on the cab enclosure, as is the ball mount for the machine gun. (Washington University)

The new ramp design, modified water boxes, and brackets for the new tow cable position are all visible here, as well as the new towing hitch and hinge protection guards. (Washington University)

Seen from the side is the first LVT(4) to be modified with the addition of the driver's side hull escape hatch. All LVT(4)s produced after this vehicle (hull number 1013A) had the hatch installed. None of the vehicles produced prior to this one was retrofitted with this feature. (Washington University)

When the hatch was in the closed position it formed a watertight seal. Ironically, the American crews usually mounted additional armor plates on the pontoons. The added plates covered this escape hatch and made it impossible to open. The crews felt that the additional armor was more advantageous than this hatch. (Washington University)

This June 1945 factory photo shows the first completed vehicle with the new side pontoon escape hatch installed. The small round device in the top half of the open hatch is the glass fitting to allow the crew inside of the vehicle to see the water level before opening this hatch. (Washington University)

The open hatches for the driver (left) and assistant driver provide a glimpse into the cab of a late LVT(4). Inside the assistant driver's hatch to the right are the watertight lockers holding the radio equipment. The curved handles on the hatch doors provided leverage to make it easier to open or close the doors. (Washington University)

Late-production features on this St. Louis Car Company LVT(4) are the rounded, tubular upper corners of the ramp in this forward-facing view. With the cover of the engine compartment bulkhead removed, the engine is visible. A towing eye is at the center of the ramp and late-type mooring posts are on the sponsons. (Washington University)

Two radio units are secured to the floor of this St. Louis Car Company LVT(4). The units comprise boxes with louvered tops and an antenna mount. Two padlocked doors are on the inboard side of each of the units. (Washington University)

The same cargo compartment and radio gear are viewed from a different angle. The swiveling pintle mount for a .30-caliber machine gun is attached to the forward end of the raised portion of the sponson. (Washington University)

Rear Admiral Clark Woodward and Vice Admiral Randall Jacobs walk by an LVT(4) while visiting the U.S. Navy's Sixth War Loan Exhibition at Chicago in December 1944. This original color image displays the Ocean Gray paint scheme of the vehicle, extending also into the cargo compartment. (Naval History and Heritage Command)

Marianas Invasion

The LVT(4) received its "Baptism of Fire" in the major landings in the Mariana Islands in 1944. The first island in the campaign was Saipan. The landings began early on the morning of 15 June 1944. At the time of the Marianas operation, the only model of the LVT(4) available to the American forces was the early unarmored version. From lessons learned in prior amphibious landings at places like Tarawa, the Marshalls, and Admiralty Islands, the amtrac crews knew they would have to add armor plating to their new LVT(4)s prior to the landings. Plates were quickly designed and manufactured from hardened steel sheets and applied to the vehicles. Because of the field expedient measures of up-armoring these vehicles the exact number of plates and their method and placement differs from vehicle to vehicle.

All of the LVT(4)s taking part in the Marianas Campaign were painted in overall Ocean Gray. Vehicle markings used on the amtracs were in the form of vertical colored stripes. The color and number of the stripes reflected their respective landing beaches. For example, a vehicle landing on Green Beach Three would have three vertical green stripes painted on its front, sides, and rear surfaces. Because the LVT(4) could conveniently carry jeeps, trailers, and artillery pieces and also quickly unload them via the rear ramp, the vehicles were held back until the third wave went in. The larger cargo compartment also made it possible to carry headquarters units and their equipment in a single vehicle, making command and control more efficient and cohesive. The addition of a series of different splash guards was also found to be necessary, since even when operating in calm seas water would often wash over the vehicle's bow and pour into the open hatches or in some cases flow over the cab roof and flood into the cargo compartment.

Amphibious vehicles assemble on a beachhead on Tinian in July 1944, including, third in line, an LVT(4) with a splash guard on top of the engine compartment. To the right is an LVT(2) with the number 20 on the unusual coaming below the machine gun shield. Next in the row is a DUKW that has seen considerable service, judging from its deteriorated paint. (National Archives)

LVT(4)s line the beach at Saipan while a load of Marines packed in an LVT(2) drives past on its way to their assigned landing beach. (USMC)

All amtracs were made of mild steel and not capable of taking the abuse that their operating environment could deliver. This vehicle apparently took a direct hit from a Japanese mortar shell while returning from the beach. (USMC)

Nine hundred yards out from the island of Saipan, a load of Marines has moved from an LCVP to an LVT(4) for the final ride to the combat beach head. As seen here, the side hull-mounted .30-caliber machine guns often had no gun shields mounted. As this vehicle nears the beach all of the passengers will hunker down to protect themselves from enemy fire. (USMC)

The rear hull-mounted ramp was manually operated by one man with a hand crank. Because of this laborious chore, many times the ramp was only lowered to the level shown here unless it required the full open position to unload cargo. The pontoon step pocket has been filled and a piece of pontoon armor plate is visible on this vehicle. (National Archives)

Issued with each vehicle, canvas tarpaulins could be used in several ways, including as ground cover to sleep on or strung from the vehicle itself to form a lean-to. With a bit of ingenuity and a few scrap pieces of wood or poles, a cover could be constructed over the vehicle's cargo compartment to shade it from the glaring tropical sun. (National Archives)

Moving inland on Saipan, this early model LVT(4) has bow armor and cab armor plates installed. These Marines have chosen to ride sitting atop the cab and bow instead of inside the cargo compartment. This could be due to the cargo compartment being full or because it is more comfortable and easier to see and exit the vehicle. Also, it was safer to be on top of the vehicle should it detonate a mine. (National Archives)

Another LVT(4) with external armor moves through the ruined streets of what is left of the business district in the city of Garapan on Saipan. This vehicle also has the splash guard added over the top rear of the front cab. The two forward .50-caliber machine guns have the one-piece flat gun shields installed. (USMC)

On Saipan, Marines unload supplies from an LVT(4) with its ramp partially lowered to a horizontal position. The fragile splash deflector has been damaged. The three vertical stripes on the side of the vehicle signified the landing beach to which it was assigned during the Saipan invasion. To the right is the front of another LVT. (USMC)

An external armor plate kit has been installed on this LVT(4) that is parked next to an LVT(A)2. Just visible at the rear of the cab roof is the splash guard added to prevent the cargo compartment from being flooded by water washing over the front cab. This LVT has both a .50- and .30-caliber machine gun but both weapons lack gun shields. (USMC)

The beach at Saipan is packed with LVT(4) amtracs and LVT(A)4 amtanks. One style of splash guard is shown in good detail on the LVT(4) in the foreground. The two round objects in front of the splash guard are the grappling hooks issued with every FMC-designed LVT, seen here in their proper stowage location. The wear and tear visible on this vehicle is quite apparent, even though this vehicle was relatively new at the time. (USMC)

31

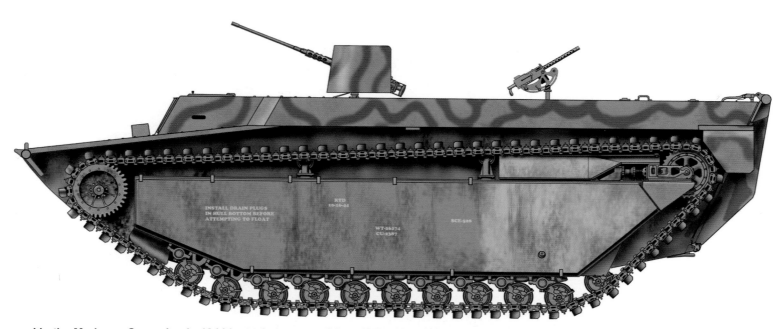

An LVT(4) that served in the Marianas Campaign in 1944 has a base coat of Ocean Gray paint, with wavy green camouflage patterns painted on the hull, omitting the pontoons. Armament includes .50-caliber machine guns with shields and .30-caliber machine guns.

LVT(4)s head along the beach at Tinian. The vehicle in the center of the photo is painted in a camouflage pattern consisting of green stripes painted over the vehicle's Ocean Gray factory finish. (USMC)

The same subject vehicle seen in the photo at left is shown here a few days later, inland on Tinian. The camouflage only appears on the vehicle's upper side surfaces and ramp face. (USMC)

Joe Blo, an LVT(4), comes ashore on Tinian on 25 July 1944, one day after D-day on that island in the Marianas. The upper hull side is bent and dented. This part of the vehicle was made from thin metal sheet and not armored steel, and therefore it was susceptible to damage. (National Archives)

Troops move from this LVT(4) to the beach on Tinian. It is unclear why they are jumping over the side of the vehicle and wading ashore. Possibly the vehicle has broken down or run out of gas. Combat damage often caused punctures in fuel tanks. (USMC)

As shown here, the LVT(4) (right) worked alongside its older, smaller brother, the LVT(2) (left) throughout World War II, though the two had different uses due to the rear ramp and larger capacity of the LVT(4). (USMC)

Columns of Marine and Army LVTs come ashore on Tinian during the Marianas Campaign in July 1944. The LVT(4) to the right with the number 22 on the ramp also bears a star, denoting a vehicle from U.S. Army stocks. Sandbags are arrayed on top of the engine compartment for extra protection. (National Archives)

LVT(2)s and LVT(4)s operate on the beach on Tinian. The ocean and beaches were the environments that the LVTs were designed to work within, when they were forced to move further inland the rougher terrain took a heavy toll on them. (National Archives)

Though the Tinian landings were a USMC operation, the U.S. Army provided the Marines with many of the amtracs from its own stocks. Army vehicles are recognized by the white star national markings painted on their exterior surfaces. (National Archives)

A number of LVT(4)s are delivering their loads to an invasion beach at Tinian. Several are backed up to the beach along the shoreline. After dropping off their cargoes, the vehicles will head back to the ships offshore to take on more loads. (USMC)

A group of LVT(4)s pause for a brief rest as they move inland on Tinian, rooting out the remnants of the Japanese forces. This early unarmored LVT(4) is painted in a zebra stripe pattern of green over Ocean Gray. (National Archives)

The suspension system of the LVTs was a relatively fragile system and could be severely damaged by even small arms and antipersonnel land mines. Here we see the damage caused by a small mine on the beach at Tinian. (USMC)

By design, LVT(4)s were not intended to be used any farther inland than landing beaches. However, they often were put to use much farther inland than intended out of necessity or convenience, such as these LVT(4)s in the Tinian operation. (USMC)

The whole point of the amphibious assault on Tinian is summarized in this scene. Seabees, numbering 15,000, built this massive airfield with six runways from which B-29s like this one could strike Japan itself. It was from Tinian that the *Enola Gay* and *Bock's Car* rose to deliver the atomic bombs, speeding the end of the war, and obviating the need for LVTs to bring troops ashore on the beaches of Japan's home islands. (Stan Piet collection)

Carolines Invasion

Operation "Stalemate," the plan to occupy the Palau Islands in September of 1944, was to be a combined USMC and U.S. Army endeavour to secure the target islands in the Carolines group. Both the Marines and Army operated the LVT(2) and LVT(4) during the battle. Again Army vehicles were given to the USMC to replace combat losses and the Army LVTs carried Marines when necessary.

The U.S. Navy sent a Flamethrower Detachment equipped with six LVT(4)s that had been converted to carry the Mk I flamethrower turret mounted in the rear cargo compartment. These six vehicles (known as flametracs), were a huge success during the battles on Peleliu and used almost constantly after their arrival. However the rough terrain on this island and the added weight of the flame unit on the lightweight unarmored vehicle demonstrated the need for a much sturdier platform for such a weapons system. This need eventually led to the design of the M4 Sherman flame tank that was used so effectively later in the war at places like Iwo Jima and Okinawa. The entire island of Peleliu was made of hard rock coral, razor sharp in some places, and this terrain quickly took its toll in men and equipment. Many of the LVTs operating on Peleliu were so beaten and damaged from enemy fire that they were no longer capable of operating in the water. They were used exclusively to deliver men and supplies to the front lines and evacuate the wounded and dead to the landing beaches. At the time of the Palaus campaign LVTs were still painted in their Ocean Gray finish, although a few vehicles carried the odd camouflage scheme and others were so weathered and covered with old overpainted markings and repair patches that they actually did appear to be camouflaged.

The Navy used numerous small craft as floating gas stations to keep the LVTs and other amphibious craft running constantly. The LVT(4) here is an early armored cab version finished in the Ocean Gray color, but numerous touch ups and heavy weathering make it almost appear as camouflaged. (National Archives)

Early armored cab model LVT(4)s loaded with Marines head for the beaches on D-Day at Peleliu. These vehicles have no gun shields installed. (USMC)

A burned out LVT(4), WTCT6A Amphibious Trailer, and a DUKW all sit on the beach at Peleliu, victims of the first day's bloody fighting. (USMC)

After the initial combat landings brought the troops ashore, the LVTs continued to serve a very important role as resupply vehicles carrying much-needed ammunition and supplies to the front lines and evacuating the wounded to the rear. This Ocean Gray early armored cab LVT(4) has the curved shields installed on its machine gun mounts. (National Archives)

This early production unarmored cab LVT(4) is sitting along the beach at Peleliu. It has the first generation add-on armor package. The front cab armor plate is shown in its lowered position. The bow plate armor can clearly be seen and all of this vehicle's machine guns have been removed. The remains of a Japanese pillbox can be seen in the foreground. (National Archives)

A burned out LVT(4) sits inland on Peleliu. An interesting detail is that the driver's side passageway to the front cab is sealed off. (National Archives)

Another burned-out wreck sitting on the beach at Peleliu. Many of these vehicles were never recovered and the remains of some can still be found there today. (USMC)

Nearly three weeks after the initial landings, big white stars identify Army vehicles – including a composite-hull M4 Sherman tank and an M29C Weasel – on the beach at Peleliu on 2 October 1944. The LVT(4)s appear to be a mix of early production unarmored versions and first production armored cab types. This is the only known photo showing the Army M29C Weasel on Peleliu; prior to this photo surfacing there was some doubt about whether the vehicle was ever used there. (Patton Museum)

A wounded Japanese POW is evacuated to a holding area. The excessive mud buildup on top of the pontoon under the tracks was a common occurrence. (USMC)

Walking wounded are boarding this LVT(4) for the short trip out to the hospital ship sitting offshore at Peleliu. (USMC)

LVTs were very often used to evacuate casualties from the front lines directly to the ships off shore, saving many lives. (USMC)

LVT(4)s sit on the beach at Peleliu waiting to be called forward. The front bow armor plate and side pontoon armor plate can clearly be seen. (National Archives)

On an invasion beach piled up with water barrels and ration boxes, several LVTs are backed-up to the shoreline, including an LVT(4) to the right. (National Archives)

One of the six U.S. Navy "flametracs" operates on Peleliu. These were mid-production armored cab versions of the LVT(4) converted to carry the Mk I flamethrower turret mounted in the rear cargo compartment. All six of these vehicles saw extensive use on Peleliu throughout the battle. Here the U.S. Navy flametracs are working with U.S. Army composite-hull M4 Sherman tanks (seen in right background) in support of USMC infantry. (National Archives)

The advance of this LVT-4 with Mark 1 flamethrower has come to a halt so Marines can remove a 200-pound mine from its path. This scene unfolded on Peleliu, where in over 61 days six Mark 1 flamethrowers were rotated among 19 LVT(4)s, eliminating 100 enemy strongholds in caves and destroying 25 bunkers. (Naval History and Heritage Command)

This is one of several LVT(4) flametracs employed on Peleliu. The vehicles mounted a Mk. 1 flamethrower and shield in the rear of the cargo compartment.

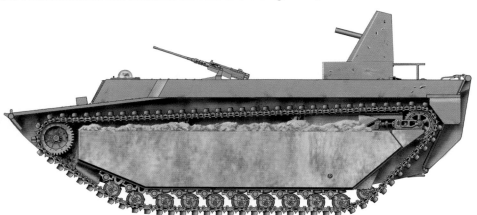

One of the most formidable weapons mounted on an amtrac was the Navy Mark 1 flamethrower. Based on the National Defense Research Committee (NDRC)-funded flamethrower manufactured by Standard Oil, work on the Navy Mark 1 was driven by fighting on Tarawa. Standard Oil and M. W. Kellogg (precursor to Kellogg, Brown and Root) manufactured 21 Mk 1 flamethrowers. The large upper tank contained 220 gallons of 7% Napalm, which was projected by Nitrogen from several 2,000-psi tanks, yielding a 100-yard range for the weapon. The 3¼-ton (each) units were designed as free-standing units capable of being mounted in landing craft. Rather than landing craft, it was decided to mount the Mark 1s on wooden palletized supporting structures, and then into LVT(4) amtracs, thereby allowing the weapon to be moved from vehicle to vehicle as required by the maintenance requirements of the LVTs. The latter would prove a significant factor, as once fielded by the Marines they tried to push far inland on Palau, stressing the amphibians to their limits due to extended rocky land operation, and severely limiting the number of vehicles available daily for combat. (National Archives via Steve Zaloga)

A rare overhead view shows one of the flametracs in operation on Peleliu, directing a stream of fire at a dug-in Japanese position. Japanese bunkers on islands like Peleliu had proved difficult to destroy with artillery fire. Hence, a few flametracs were brought along for the Peleliu invasion to deal with such fortifications. (National Archives)

A closer view of one of the flametracs in action. The vehicle has green stripes with black outlines painted over its original, though weather-beaten, Ocean Gray finish. The vehicle has lost its rear water boxes and appears to have an extra .50-caliber Browning machine gun mounted directly to the right of the flame turret. (National Archives)

A front view of one of the flametracs operating on Peleliu. This vehicle has the factory produced add-on armor kit installed and lacks gun shields. (USMC)

The white cross seen on the flame guns front shield is actually open space for the operator to see through when aiming the weapon. (USMC)

Army amtracs are used to carry Marines across the shallow causeway connecting Ngesebus Island to Peleliu. This vehicle has the flat-style gun shields on the forward machine guns. The left gun is manned by one of the LVT crewmen and the right gun is manned by one of the Marines being transported. The vehicle's registration number is painted in large white numerals on the rear ramp and it appears that older markings have been painted out along with the white star on the ramp. Sometimes the stars were simply covered with a coating of grease to hide them. (USMC)

U.S. Army cannon-armed amtracs visible in the distance lead the assault on Ngesebus (modern Ngedbus) in advance of the LVT(4), one of which stands by in the foreground. This LVT(4) has U.S. Army markings and the registration number 996269 in white on the ramp. A small banner is flying from the whip antenna. (National Archives)

Hitting the beach under light enemy fire, the amtracs prepare to unload their Marine cargo so they can move forward to engage the Japanese in battle. (USMC)

Army troops of the 81st Infantry Division ride ashore on an early unarmored LVT(4). They are a part of the invasion force that landed on the Ulithi Atoll in the Caroline Islands on 23 September 1944. (National Archives)

The fighting over, Marines prepare to head back to Peleliu after turning Ngesebus over to the Army. The LVT(4) in the background has a canvas roof covering the cargo compartment. (USMC)

An Army patrol is taken inland aboard an LVT(4) on Luzon in the Philippines on 19 January 1945. The initial landings were met by very little opposition. The Ocean Gray paint is weathered to a chalky appearance. (USMC)

A late production LVT(4) passes the hulks of two Japanese E13A Aichi float planes at Puerto Princesa on Palawan Island in the Philippines on 1 March 1945. Cargo is being unloaded from LSMs in the background. (National Archives)

Marines and equipment clutter the shoreline as an LVT(4) burns in the background. Even with the additional armored protection added the LVT was extremely vulnerable to Japanese artillery and mortar rounds. (USMC)

A late production LVT(4) disappears into a thick mangrove swamp on the coastline of the Palawan Islands, 28 February 1945. The soldiers are members of "E" Company, 180th Infantry, 41st Division. (National Archives)

Sailors watch from the bow of an LST as an early production Army LVT(4) is backed aboard in preparation for the Luzon landings in January 1945. An LST could carry 20 M4 Medium Tanks. (Quartermaster Museum)

More than a weapon of war, the original LVTs were designed to serve as logistical vehicles to transport troops and supplies to the beach from the ships offshore. It was only later that they were seen as assault vehicles and were so armed and armored. (National Archives)

Fittingly, given the Alligator's origin as an evacuation vehicle, this LVT(4) is evacuating wounded civilian personnel. Many wounded were saved because of the speed at which they could reach the medical facilities floating off shore of any given invasion beach. (National Archives)

Troops of the 41st Division walk out the back of a LVT(4) on the rocky shore of Palawan Island. The advantage of the dropping rear ramp of this model amtrac, compared to earlier models which required troops to clamber over the side or rear, is plainly evident. (National Archives)

A smoke screen laid by ships is beginning to drift across White Beach Two as a pair of LVT(4)s come ashore in the Lingayen Gulf, Philippines, on 9 January 1945. Both are equipped with M36B shields protecting the .50-caliber gunner behind the driver. (National Archives)

Rivers were often used as highways to travel inland to remote villages and deliver troops and supplies. Most Filipinos greatly appreciated the supplies and support that were given to them by the American forces. In return they supplied U.S. forces with invaluable intelligence. (National Archives)

Though not designed to work far inland of the assault beaches, LVTs were often called upon to carry troops and supplies to the front as it moved inland. This colorful LVT(4) approaches the outskirts of Manila in February 1945. (USMC)

G.I.s, including several on top of the LVT(4) to the right, look on while combat engineers deal with a Japanese booby trap buried in the middle of a road in the Philippine Islands toward the end of World War II. The vehicle's name is *Pleasant Moments* and a pin-up girl adorns the side of the box-style gun shield. (National Archives)

A first production armored cab variant of LVT(4) passes a group of recently liberated Philippine civilians cheering on the U.S. advance. The bolted-on bow armor plate clearly shows the wear and tear that these vehicles went through. (USMC)

Iwo Jima Invasion

By the time of the Iwo Jima operation in February of 1945, the Japanese had adopted a strong defense-in-depth strategy. Because of this, the Marines who assaulted Iwo Jima were forced to fight with utmost savagery for every inch of the contested island.

After an intense bombardment by the Navy, joined by Army Air Force bombers, Marines began to move toward the shore in LVTs. Sixty-eight of the LVTs were cannon-armed LVT(A)4s, which were followed by a mixture of LVT(4) and LVT(2) types, totaling 380 troop-carrying amtracs. The LVTs reached the black sand of the Iwo Jima beaches within two minutes of H-Hour. The sand caused immediate problems, with some LVTs sinking to their bellies and becoming mired. With their ramps lowered, the crashing waves soon filled the amtracs, many of them broaching.

Multi-color camouflage schemes began appearing on LVTs at Iwo Jima, although plain-Jane overall Ocean Gray LVTs operated side-by-side with the camouflaged vehicles. Early unarmored, add-on armor, and the first of the armored cab versions all were used during the battle. Both the early flat and later curved style of gun shields were used. Markings on the amtracs were the standard colored stripes, the number and color denoting the assigned landing beaches. For example, a vehicle landing on Red Beach #2 would have two red stripes painted on its sides, rear ramp, and front cab. The size of the stripes varied quite a bit from unit to unit. Other markings such as the company (A, B, C, D, etc) and vehicle number within the company were usually also painted on all four sides of the vehicle.

An overhead view of an early up-armored LVT(4) leaving an LST at Iwo Jima. Curved gun shields and a small splash guard are visible on the cab roof. (National Archives)

The first wave of amtracs makes a run for the landing beaches at Iwo Jima on 19 February 1945. Each of the two LVT(4)s in the foreground has two .50-caliber machine gun mounts with curved armor shields. The vehicle on the left bears the number 79 on the cab, while the one to the right is 78. (National Archives)

Troop-laden LVT(4)s head for the invasion beaches at Iwo Jima on D-Day, 19 February 1945. Navy ships are blasting Mt. Suribachi in the background. (Natioanl Archives)

A Marine LVT(4) equipped with the early curved machine gun shields swims ashore during the Iwo Jima landings. A U.S. Navy *Cleveland*-class cruiser shells Japanese shore positions in the distance. (National Archives)

A line of LVTs churn through the surf during the landings on Iwo Jima. Smoke from the naval bombardment is evident above the shoreline. The colored stripes are evident on the sponson and ramp of the central LVT(4). (National Archives)

A Marine Corps LVT(4) equipped with a wide splash rail and round machine gun shields is launched from an LST off Iwo Jima in February 1945. The crew of LST 787 was made up of members of the U.S. Coast Guard. (National Archives)

The driver of an LVT named *Carolyn* on an Iwo Jima beach in February of 1945 operates the controls from outside the hatch to gently maneuver the vehicle down the ramp of an LCT. (National Archives)

The wrecked hulks of vehicles, amtracs, and landing craft along with bodies of slain Marines litter the beach of Iwo Jima following the landings. The LVT(4) wears bands of green paint over its base gray. (National Archives)

Camouflaged Marine LVTs move inland on Iwo Jima in the rain. The crew of the forward vehicle has added sand bags to protect the unarmored cab. The second vehicle is equipped with an armor kit. (National Archives)

This LVT(4) is being unloaded on the beach at Iwo. The cargo is still contained in the net in which it was transferred from the ship to the amtrac. (National Archives)

This LVT(4) is unloading its load of ammunition to a forward supply depot located just behind the front lines on Iwo. (National Archives)

LVTs carrying members of the 4th Marine Division stream toward the landing beaches of Iwo Jima on D-day. In the foreground is a camouflage-painted, early-model LVT(4). (National Archives)

A camouflaged LVT(4) loaded with Marines stops next to a Navy support ship before heading into the beach. (National Archives)

A single-color early armored cab LVT(4) moves towards the beach on D-Day morning. This vehicle has the early flat style of machine gun shields. (National Archives)

Marines transfer from an LVT(4) into an LCVP for the ride into the beaches at Iwo Jima. One of the LCVP crew is using a boat hook to help stabilize the two craft. (National Archives)

An early unarmored variant of the LVT(4), with the first generation up-armored kit package installed. One of the crewmen is sitting on one of the field-modified type of splash guards mounted atop the cab. The crewmen also wear "Mae West"-style flotation vests due to the fact that the earlier Kapok life vests were too bulky to wear when operating within the tight confines of the LVT cabs. This vehicle carries the curved style machine gun shields. (National Archives)

An LVT(4) has come ashore on Iwo Jima, and its bilge pumps are still expelling water from the discharge pipes running across the front end of the hull. On the pontoon is stenciled the number A43, next to which is a stripe indicating the assigned landing beach. The crewmen are wearing hooded waterproof outerwear. (National Archives)

As soon as the first wave of LVT(4)s delivered the Marines to the island, they began evacuating casualties. There is a splash guard on top of this early armored-cab LVT(4). (National Archives)

An ammunition dump explodes in the distance, beyond the LVT(4) in the foreground, on Iwo Jima on 21 February 1945. The vehicle has at least one darker camouflage color applied over its base color, and A29 is stenciled at the center of the pontoon. Crates and five-gallon liquid containers are stacked inside the cargo compartment. (National Archives)

On a beachhead at Iwo Jima during the battle, the closest LVT(4) is an early unarmored version with add-on armor plates installed. The vehicle next to it is an unusual field conversion of a first-model, armored-cab LVT(4) with a plywood enclosure with windows. This may have been some type of command vehicle or possibly an engineer maintenance or shop vehicle. (National Archives)

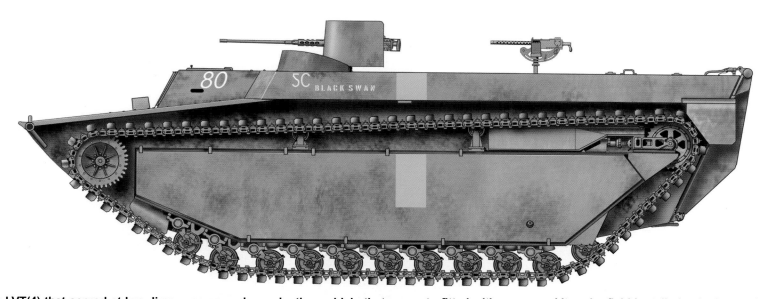

The Black Swan, an LVT(4) that served at Iwo Jima, was an early-production vehicle that was retrofitted with an armor kit and a field-installed splash guard atop the engine-compartment roof. Yellow stripes on the vehicle indicated it was assigned to the Yellow Beach landings.

The Black Swan, named after a pirate ship in a Tyrone Power movie of the same name, lies abandoned on the beach at Iwo Jima. This early production unarmored LVT(4) has been uparmored with one of the early add-on armor packages. This vehicle also carries a field-designed splash guard to keep water from splashing over the front cab and flooding the cargo compartment. (National Archives)

In a scene evocative of the savage, hard-fought invasion of Iwo Jima, an LVT(A)4 armed with a 75mm howitzer in a turret sits in the surf in front of a destroyed Japanese ship along the 4th Marine Division's beachhead, while in the background, camouflage-painted LVT(4)s come ashore and pick their way through the debris and wreckage on the beach, heading for cover below the bench paralleling the shore. (National Archives)

Disabled and destroyed amtracs litter the volcanic sand on the beachhead at Iwo Jima, while an apparently still-operational LVT(4) sits to the left. In the foreground are three abandoned LVT(4)s, while partially buried in the sand beyond them is an LVT(A)4. In the background are the bunkers and tents of the invading Marines. (National Archives)

Okinawa Invasion

Okinawa was the final and largest amphibious operation of WWII. After the bloody victories America had recently won over the Japanese at Peleliu and Iwo Jima, planners of the Okinawa operations were expecting more of the same. But the Japanese had decided to change their tactics to one of not contesting the landings at all and allowing the American forces to move far inland before being ambushed and attacked in force. Due to this Japanese ploy, many vehicles, including the LVT(4), not designed or intended for use in the front lines, found themselves in the thick of the fighting, sometimes with devastating results.

Okinawa saw the use of the largest number and types of LVT(4) in all of WWII. Everything from the first unarmored models to the mid-production initial armored cab version to the late production armored cab variant took part in the battle. A new armored "Box" style of machine gun shield was introduced as well. The U.S. Army began receiving LVT(4)s painted in overall Olive Drab, although the USMC was still using the Ocean Gray or camouflaged vehicles. Marine replacement vehicles coming from Army stocks would have been the only olive drab LVT(4)s used by the USMC during Okinawa.

Markings on the amtracs were the standard colored stripes, the number and color denoting the assigned landing beaches. For example, a vehicle landing on Red Beach #2 would have two red stripes painted on its sides, rear ramp, and front cab. The size of the stripes varied quite a bit from unit to unit. Other markings such as the company (A, B, C, D, etc.,) and vehicle number within the company were usually also painted on all four sides of the vehicle.

A mid-production armored cab LVT(4) leaves its LST with a load of Marines heading for the invasion beaches on Okinawa. (National Archives)

An LVT(4), registration number 59800, carries Army infantrymen off the ramp of a landing ship, tank (LST) during the invasion of Iheya Jima, off the coast of Okinawa, on 3 June 1945. The aim of this operation was to seize a location to install long-range radar and fighter-director stations to support the Okinawa invasion. (National Archives)

An LVT(4) backs up to a landing craft off Okinawa to take on a fresh load of cargo for delivery to an invasion beach on Okinawa. Two crewmen wearing life jackets are visible on the amtrac. (National Archives)

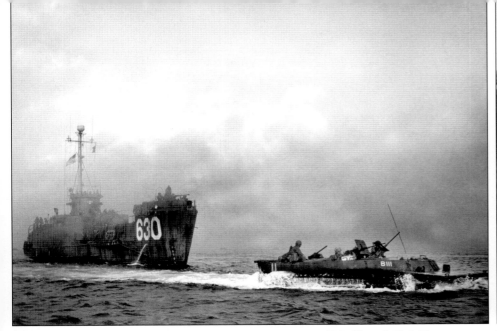

Off Okinawa, a camouflage-painted LVT(4) churns past a U.S. Navy LCI, taking a group of Marines ashore. The invasion of Okinawa, or Operation Iceberg, was a massive undertaking that employed vast numbers of amtracs. (National Archives)

Troops are crowded in an LVT(4) during the invasion of Okinawa. To the left are the grab-handles of a row of five-gallon liquid containers, while to the right are visible an early-style mooring post and several grab-handles on top of the sponson. An M2 .50-caliber machine gun completes the scene. (National Archives)

The 8th Marines consolidate their beachhead after landing on Iheya Jima without opposition on 3 June 1945. The landing force had sustained a few minor casualties from friendly fire during the pre-landing naval bombardment of the island. The nearest vehicle is an LVT(4), seen from aft. Other amtracs are in the distance. (National Archives)

Two early-style armored-cab LVT(4)s come ashore on Okinawa. The vehicle on the left has the new-style box gun shields while the others have the field-fabricated curved gun shields. (National Archives)

This late-production, armored LVT(4), which saw action in the Battle of Okinawa in 1945, featured an overall Olive Drab paint scheme and a white recognition star on the pontoon, indicating that the amtrac originated from U.S. Army inventory. Two .50-caliber machine guns were mounted with box-type shields. Two red stripes indicate this vehicle was assigned to Red Beach Two.

A U.S. Army early-type LVT(4) with varied markings, including *I Walk Alone* surrounded by little white footprints and the code "A108" on the side of the sponson, heads for shore at Okinawa. Felix the Cat is painted on the sponson toward the front. *Leyte* and the Phillipines campaign ribbon is painted on the cab front. (National Archives)

According to the original caption of this possibly posed photo, it is L-Day on Okinawa, 1 April 1945, and Marines are hitting Blue Beach 2. The LVT(4) bears the nickname *The Memphis Belle* and a camouflage paint scheme, including a light-colored patch on the lower front of the hull. A large tow hook is attached to the vehicle. (National Archives)

Rooster, an early production unarmored cab vehicle that has had externally mounted armor plating added to the cab front in the field, comes ashore at Okinawa. This vehicle has a large colorful dragon/sea monster painted on its lower front bow. No sponson side armor plating is mounted at all but it does carry the full complement of four machine guns. (USMC)

A multicolor-camouflaged early-production LVT(4) rests on the shoreline on Okinawa. In this campaign, camouflage colors for these amtracs typically included green, dark brown, beige or tan, and sometimes black. No machine guns are mounted on the vehicle, suggesting that the photo was taken late in the Okinawa campaign, when the fighting had moved far inland. (National Archives)

Marines of the 6th Division cast their shadows on a destroyed LVT(4) as they advance toward the southern tip of Okinawa. The spot where a Japanese antitank round struck the vehicle is visible on the pontoon. The track was also severed and is hanging from the idler, providing a close-up view of the W-shaped cleats. (National Archives)

This LVT(4) barely made it to shore before it was destroyed. The aft port sponson was peeled back, exposing part of the cargo compartment to view. Amid the twisted wreckage are the machine guns, which usually were salvaged as soon as possible if still in working condition. A curved gun shield is also present. (USMC)

Amtracs come ashore on L-Day on Okinawa, 1 April 1945. To the lower right is an LVT(A)4, with a 75mm howitzer that could provide close support for the landing force. In the background are several LVT(4)s with curved gun shields. The ramp of the vehicle to the left is lowered, and Marines are hunkered down to the rear of the vehicles. (National Archives)

Marine LVT(4)s come ashore on Okinawa with reinforcements on 3 June 1945. The vehicle on the left has the early armored cab with a hinged door over the driver's front window. A protective Plexiglas dome is present over the periscope in the assistant driver's escape hatch door. (National Archives)

Second-wave troops who have arrived in LVT(4)s assemble behind a seawall at a beachhead on Okinawa. The vehicles have varying patterns of camouflage paint, and some have more than one color applied over the base color. Individual vehicle numbers are painted in a light color on each side of the cabs. (National Archives)

In this view of part of the landing beaches on the island of Iheya Shima, the nearest LVT(4) clearly shows the convenience of the rear ramp for loading and unloading cargo such as this power generator trailer. Several LVT(3)s in the background have canvas covers stretched over their cargo compartments to provide protection from the noonday sun. (National Archives)

Personnel ride atop an LVT(4) on Okinawa. The driver is in his open escape hatch. This vehicle has the early-type armored cab and armor on the front of the hull. To the right are several WTCT-6A amphibious trailers. With their boat-shaped bows and watertight construction, they could be drawn through water behind amtracs. (National Archives)

Parked behind amtrac crewmen posing with sanshin, traditional three-stringed Okinawan instruments, is an LVT(4) in a three-color camouflage scheme, splotches of red brown, forest green, and a whitish-cream tan over the original, very faded Ocean Gray. (USMC)

When conditions became too muddy for wheeled cargo vehicles to operate, as in this photo taken in May 1945 during the Battle of Okinawa, amtracs such as the LVT(4) at the center could deliver men and supplies where needed, as long as the mud was not too deep. This vehicle has the marking 1-B-49 on the extension above the top of the ramp. (National Archives)

Blood & Guts is an ex-Army LVT(4) that has been turned over to the Marines on Okinawa. The side hull white stars have been painted over but they left the star on the front hull top to help prevent allied aircraft from mistaking the vehicle for a Japanese one. (USMC)

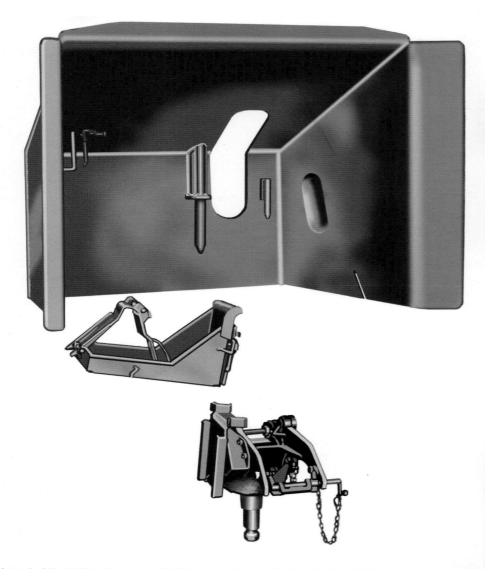

This LVT(4) on Okinawa has the new M69E box-style gun shields and is painted in a three-color camouflage scheme. The area on top of the side pontoon and below the top run of tracks has filled with dirt and sand. The crew of the amtrac are cleaning the stretchers it is carrying for use in evacuating battlefield casualties. (National Archives)

Drums of fuel are being unloaded from this LVT(4) that has box-style machine gun shields. This operation was much more difficult on earlier LVTs that had no rear ramp. (National Archives)

Late in World War II, many LVT(4)s began to be fitted with the M69E shielded bracket mount, also sometimes known as 7069694, shown here in this illustration from ORD 9 SNL A-75. The shield itself was designated part number 7069692, and it provided protection from splinters and low-velocity projectiles from the front and sides, as well as somewhat from plunging fire from the upper front. The opening for the machine gun was offset to the right side of the shield. Shown below the shield are the tray assembly for the .50-caliber ammunition box, part number D90078, and the cradle and pintle assembly, part number 7069693, which held the machine gun and allowed it to rotate on its pedestal mount as well as to elevate and depress on the cradle.

64

Pieces of bamboo have been cut and placed onto the top edge of these flat gun shields, a feature seen on quite a few vehicles. It is possibly a form of padding to shield the sharp edge. (National Archives)

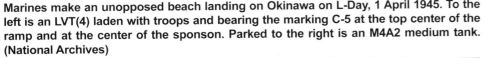

Marines make an unopposed beach landing on Okinawa on L-Day, 1 April 1945. To the left is an LVT(4) laden with troops and bearing the marking C-5 at the top center of the ramp and at the center of the sponson. Parked to the right is an M4A2 medium tank. (National Archives)

Here we see the more common curved gun shields, originally developed for use on the earlier LVT(A)2 series of amtracs. The gun on the right is a .50-caliber machine gun while the left-hand gun is a .30-caliber model. (National Archives)

One of the most savage phases of the Battle of Okinawa was the struggle for heavily defended Sugar Loaf Hill. In this view from the hill, an LVT(4) is in the center background, while to the right, in front of an M4 medium tank, is an LVT(3). This snub-nosed amtrac made its operational debut during the Okinawa invasion. (National Archives)

These Army LVT(4)s are operating in support of USMC infantry late in the battle for Okinawa. The large white stars painted on the vehicles are a trait identifying them as U.S. Army vehicles. (National Archives)

The Army LVT(4) is an early production model with the first armored cab and a two-piece appliqué armor package on the sponson sides to protect the rear gas tank and the front drivers' area. (National Archives)

The crew of this LVT(4) are performing maintenance on their amtrac late in the Okinawa campaign. Two of the men are standing on one of the "Box"-type machine gun shields as they tend to the tracks. The barefoot crewman has the big toe of his left foot resting inside the main fuel tank drain plug fitting access point. (National Archives)

A U.S. Army LVT(4) has just delivered a group of Marines to a beach at Okinawa. The vehicle is painted overall Olive Drab. While the U.S. Army painted the white star on its LVTs in World War II, the Marines did not. A pin-up girl has been painted on the side of the M69E gun shield. (National Archives)

An Army LVT(4) carries a load of Army troops to the beach at Okinawa. Many of the passengers are wearing "Kapok" style flotation vests and standard M1 helmets with no cloth covers. Two armor panels are visible on the pontoon side, one to protect the fuel tank and the other to protect the front cab crew. (National Archives)

Cargo is unloaded from LVT(4)s at one of the many supply depots on Okinawa. Because the machine guns are still mounted on these amtracs, it is likely that the battle was still being fought when the photo was taken. The nearest amtrac is an early armored-cab model with a splash guard in front of the cab. Behind it is an early unarmored model with an add-on armor kit. (National Archives)

LVT(4)s, including the Army vehicle with a white star, are parked on the landing beach at Iheya Shima during the invasion of that island off the coast of Okinawa. (National Archives)

The landings on Iheya Shima were unopposed and the lack of any opposition made for an eerie and uncomfortable experience for American forces. (National Archives)

LVT(4) SPECIFICATIONS

ENGINE DATA

ENGINE MAKE/MODEL*
Continental W670-9A
NUMBER OF CYLINDERS
Radial 7 cylinders
DISPLACEMENT
668 Cubic inches
HORSEPOWER
250 @ 2,400 r.p.m.
TORQUE
578 @ 1,600 r.p.m.
GOVERNED SPEED
2,400 r.p.m.

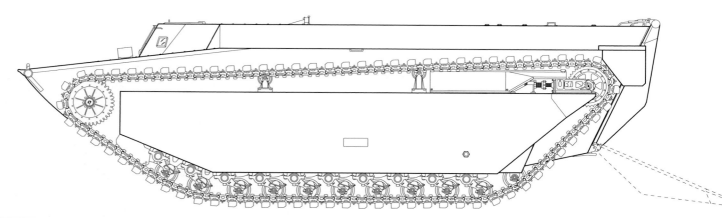

MODEL	LVT(4)
FIGHTING WEIGHT	36,400 pounds
LENGTH (main gun forward)	314 inches
WIDTH	128 inches
HEIGHT	98.5 inches
TRACK	114 inches
STD TRACK WIDTH	14 inches
ELECTRICAL	12 volt negative ground

MAXIMUM SPEED	
LAND	15 m.p.h.
WATER	7 m.p.h.
FUEL CAPACITY	140 gallons
RANGE	
LAND	150 miles
WATER	100 miles
TURNING RADIUS	30 feet

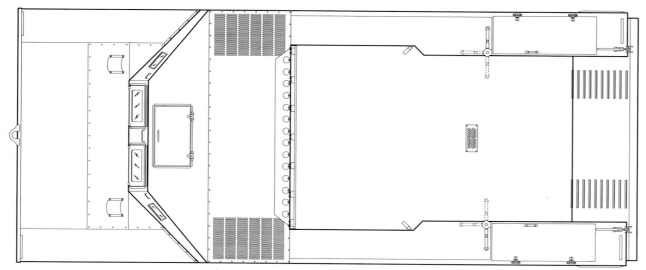

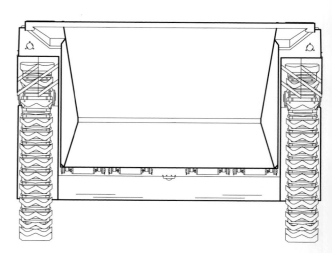

Europe and Postwar

The use of LVTs in Europe was quite limited when compared to the massive amphibious operations undertaken all through the Pacific war in WWII. All models of amtrac saw service in Europe and North Africa. The LVT(4) was used in Italy, Belgium, and Germany, mostly for river crossings.

The only use of LVTs in their designed role of amphibious assault from ships offshore to the invasion beaches was the LVT(1)s in North Africa. Photos do show LVT(1)s and LVT(2)s sitting on the beaches at Normandy, however they appear to of been used in very small numbers only after the beaches were secured, possibly by engineers.

After WWII, the LVT(4) continued to serve with distinction with several foreign armies. While America switched over to the Borg-Warner-produced LVT(3) for its amtrac of choice from 1946 through the mid-1950s, the French used the LVT(4) extensively during their war in Indochina. These vehicles had a fair number of conversions for French use, such as folding wooden bench seats, modified headlights and guards, a left-side pontoon face-mounted escape hatch and minor changes added to the late production armored cab.

The French also modified some LVT(4)s to carry a 40mm Bofors gun in a revolving turret. This feature proved a very effective weapons system when the vehicle saw service in Indochina and the Middle East. Spain, Nationalist China, and Argentina were a few of the countries to use the LVT(4) into the 1950s.

A full load of infantry from the U.S. Army's 3rd Battalion, 351st Infantry Regiment, 88th Infantry Division are being transported across the Po River in Ostiglia, Italy, on 24 April 1945. This vehicle has the late-production single-post mooring posts; consequently, it also has the late-model armored cab. The box-style machine gun shields are shown to good advantage. (National Archives)

Troops of the U.S. Army's 6th Armored Division check over an LVT(4) at Vallette, France, on 7 December 1944. Visible at the front and rear of the pontoon are two appliqué armor panels. The cab is the early armored type with no side vision device for the driver. On the driver's escape hatch is a Plexiglas periscope cover. (National Archives)

A pair of early production armored cab LVT(4)s arrive for the 6th Armored Division to use in upcoming river crossings in France during December 1944. (National Archives)

An LVT(4) crosses a river in Italy in 1945. One of the front box-type machine gun shields has been moved back to one of the side-mounted machine gun positions. (National Archives)

U.S. Army infantrymen are preparing to load into these early armored-cab LVT(4)s on the banks of a river in Italy in 1945. There is a platform for the gunner on the middle vehicle. (National Archives)

This early model armored cab LVT(4) seen in Europe during WWII is finished in the Ocean Gray overall paint scheme. The interior of the hatches are painted in gloss white, unlike armored vehicles in WWII. (National Archives)

This photo illustrates the reason that the earlier LVTs needed to be modified. Carrying a cargo like this artillery piece would have been nearly impossible without the rear ramp and larger cargo compartment of the LVT(4). (National Archives)

An LVT(4) with armored plates on the sponsons is loaded with both a jeep and a 57mm antitank gun to test the ability to ferry them. LVTs were relatively rare vehicles with U.S. troops in Northwest Europe. (US Army Engineer History Office)

An unarmored LVT(4) carries a 105mm howitzer across a river somewhere in Europe, its barrel protected by a life vest. The paint appears to have been touched up in areas with fresh olive drab paint. (US Army Engineer History Office)

Paratroopers of the 505th Parachute Infantry Regiment, 82nd Airborne Division, ride a British-operated Buffalo IV up onto the east bank of the Elbe River at Bleckede, Germany, on 30 April 1945. (National Archives)

Members of the 737th Tank Battalion, attached to the 35th Infantry Division, experiment with driving an LVT(4) on a body of water somewhere in Europe in 1944. The man holding the boat hook is wearing a tanker's helmet and jacket. (National Archives)

The great bulkiness of the LVT(4) and its low, enclosed cab tended to make visibility difficult for the driver. Many times, experienced drivers were observed executing delicate maneuvers from a position outside of the hatch, operating the steering levers with their legs. (U.S. Army Engineer History Office)

Scores of LVT(4)s are gathered in a vehicle park outside Pisa Italy after the war. A number of the vehicles mount racks built from angle iron to support log mats, or fascines, used for traversing very soft ground. (Patton Museum)

These LVTs have been stripped and deposited in the vehicle park in Italy. Thousands of vehicles were gathered in similar parks around the world at the war's end to be scrapped, their usefulness at an end. (Patton Museum)

The British modified this late LVT(4), registration number 346613, with two flamethrowers in shielded mounts and a machine gun cupola at the cargo compartment rear. Dubbed the *Sea Serpent,* it was earmarked for the 34th Amphibian Support Regiment, Royal Marines, to use in East Asia, but the war ended before it saw combat. (The Tank Museum)

The same *Sea Serpent* shown on the preceding page is viewed from aft, revealing the rears of the flamethrowers and their shields. The rounded upper corners of the ramp were a late-production feature of the LVT(4). This type of flamethrower amtrac was intended to operate in teams with LVT(4)s equipped with Hedgehog rocket launchers. (The Tank Museum)

British LVT(4) Buffalos, some with box-shaped gun shields and some without, assemble on a field in Europe. On top of the engine compartment on each vehicle is a Polsten 20mm cannon. Each LVT(4) has two Browning M2 .50-caliber machine guns with armored shields. An aimable smoke discharger is present at each forward corner of the cargo compartment on these vehicles. (The Tank Museum)

A column of British or Canadian amtracs crosses a misty European field. The Buffalo IV on the left, and probably others in the column, mounts a 20mm Polsten cannon atop the engine compartment. This vehicle, with "57" on the side of the cab, also has one machine gun shield, on the port side of the cargo compartment. (The Tank Museum)

A British or Canadian LVT(4) crosses a river in Europe toward the end of World War II. In British service, the LVT(4) was designated the Buffalo IV. This example is filled with troops, and it is difficult to determine what armaments the vehicle mounted. To the right is another amphibious vehicle used by the British, the DUKW. (The Tank Museum)

British Tommies clamber up the side of a Buffalo IV of the 4th Royal Tank Regiment during the Rhine River crossing on 24 March 1945. The insignia of the British 79th Armoured Division is on the left side of the ramp, which apparently is not operable because the top of the ramp is supporting an arrangement of slats for stowing equipment. (The Tank Museum)

Coming ashore on the eastern bank of the Rhine on 24 March 1945, a Buffalo IV takes part in Operation Plunder, the crossing of the Rhine by the British Second Army and U.S. Ninth Army that had begun the preceding night. The British 33rd Armoured Brigade of the 79th Armoured Division made the crossing in Buffalo IVs. (The Tank Museum)

Bearing the vehicle number 58 on the side of the cab, a Buffalo IV emerges from a river. Sections of rubber tires have been fitted over the front corners of the vehicle, evidently as bumpers. A 20mm Polsten cannon, a Browning .30-caliber machine gun, a smoke discharger, and at least three radio antennas are visible on the vehicle. (The Tank Museum)

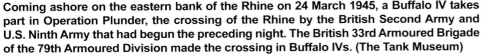

As a Buffalo IV bearing vehicle number 22 on its ramp enters the water, two men in the cargo compartment hold onto a large, indistinct structure, which, on close examination, does not appear to be machine gun shields. Allocations of Buffalo IVs to the 79th Armoured Division varied over time; in early 1945, 72 were allotted per regiment. (The Tank Museum)

The machine gun shields on this Buffalo IV, vehicle number 69, are significantly lighter in color than the hull. Faintly visible on the upper forward part of the pontoon is the illegible registration number. Troops are dismounting from the other Buffalo IV in the background; that vehicle appears to lack machine gun shields. (The Tank Museum)

A jeep is unloaded from a Buffalo IV of the 4th Royal Tank Regiment during Operation Plunder, the crossing of the Rhine on 24 March 1945. On the amtrac to the left, a smoke discharger is visible to the left of the right gun shield. The Buffalo IV to the right has the number 8F painted on its sponson in outline. (The Tank Museum)

A British 6-pounder antitank gun is secured in the cargo compartment of a Buffalo IV, ready for transport. A clear view is provided of the interior of the ramp and its nonskid slats. Also in view are the slots on the rear of the hull to accommodate the ramp cables. The splash deflectors, which were fragile and prone to being bent or broken, are intact. (The Tank Museum)

Troops manhandle equipment, possibly a trailer, from a Buffalo IV, while the same Buffalo IV numbered 8F shown in the preceding photo still stands by to the right. The shield on the .30-caliber machine gun on the starboard side of the cargo hold appears to have no gun slot. A Polsten gun mount and a .50-caliber machine gun are also present. (The Tank Museum)

Although the Buffalo IV could accommodate a 6-pounder gun or 25-pounder howitzer in its cargo compartment, the 17-pounder antitank gun would not fit. The British therefore devised a way to transport a towed 17-pounder atop the Buffalo IV, by fitting the vehicle with ramps to accommodate the gun, as seen in this frontal view. (The Tank Museum)

Next, trussed ramps are fitted to the front of the hull and extending to the ground. Here, preparations are underway to pull a 17-pounder antitank gun up the ramps to the top of the vehicle. More properly designated the Ordnance Quick-firing (QF) 17-pounder, many consider this powerful weapon the best Allied antitank gun of World War II. (The Tank Museum)

The Ordnance QF 17-pounder is secured to the ramp atop the Buffalo IV and is pointing aft as the vehicle makes its way through the water. The 17-pounder and its carriage weighed approximately 6,000 pounds; transporting this weapon on top of a relatively small amphibious vehicle would have required great caution and calm waters. (The Tank Museum)

One of the special-purpose modifications the British performed on Buffalo IVs was mounting an apparatus for carrying and laying down rolls of chespale matting, to enable following vehicles to negotiate soft or slippery ground. The matting was formed from tough fabric secured to lateral bars, which were connected together with twisted wire. (The Tank Museum)

Crewmen wrestle with a roll of chespale matting atop a Buffalo IV. The cradle that held the roll over the front of the vehicle was made of angle irons. During the Operation Plunder crossing of the Rhine, several British amtracs crossed the river in advance of the tanks and laid down chespale on the east bank, to prepare a path for the tanks. (The Tank Museum)

On the coast of Thule, Greenland, a Caterpillar bulldozer prepares the beach to allow the tracked crane to offload cargo from an LCU. The LVT(4) will be used to haul the drums inland. (US Army Transportation Museum)

U.S. Army troops conduct amphibious exercises on the coast of California on 18 November 1952. The LVT and LCM landing craft are WWII era equipment. The LVT still mounts the box-type machine gun shields. (US Army Transportation Museum)

LST 561's bow ramp is extended to launch an LVT(4) on a beach inside the Arctic Circle. The construction from 1947-1955 of the DEW Line radar warning network required vehicles with unique abilities to supply the sites. (US Army Transportation Museum)

A tracked crane is used to remove cargo from an LCU on the coast of Thule, Greenland, in 1956. The original design intent of the LVT series vehicles for logistics use was utilized for many mundane postwar chores. (US Army Transportation Museum)

Fuel drums are unloaded from an LCU on the beaches of Greenland during Operation Dewline. An Army LVT(4) *Lone Wolf* is prepared to move the fuel ashore. The machine gun is missing from the ball mount. (US Army Transportation Museum)

A late production LVT(4) with the port side escape hatch comes ashore past an LCU during the DEW Line Operations. Each member of the crew appears to have marked the vehicle with large personal names. (US Army Transportation Museum)

Late Production LVT(4)s of the 3rd Marine Division land on the beach of Okinawa for maneuvers in June of 1954. The two machine guns mounted are .30-caliber Brownings with small armored shields. (National Archives)

Although the LVT series was designed with amphibious operations in mind, its performance in snow is excellent as well. The low ground pressure provides good flotation, the track cleats great traction. (USMC)

In a photograph that seems at first glance almost like a bizarre photomontage, several aircraft, including a B-24 Liberator to the right, hover over a graveyard of junked vehicles on a Pacific island, including several amtracs: two partially intact ones are at the center, and one is at the bottom. At the end of World War II, the United States armed forces deemed it more expedient to destroy much of its surplus equipment overseas than to go to the expense and effort of transporting it home. This was an ignominious end for the hard-working, dependable, but, in the end, expendable amphibious tractors. From the germ of an idea of Donald Roebling in the 1930s had developed a series of vehicles that enabled the United States to pursue its strategy of island-hopping and claim victory in the Pacific. (Stan Piet collection)